ROCKS and Minerals

by Lindsay A. Caputo

sundance™

sundance™

Program written and developed by Kate Boehm Jerome
in association with Sundance Publishing.

Editorial, Design, and Production by Baseline Development Group
in association with Sundance Publishing.

Consultant/Reviewer: Rebecca L. Johnson, Science Writer, Sioux Falls, SD

Published by
Sundance Publishing, LLC
33 Boston Post Road West
Suite 440
Marlborough, MA 01752
800-343-8204
www.sundancepub.com

Photography:
Cover Roberto de Gugliemo/Photo Researchers, Inc.; p. 1 James Blank/Index Stock Imagery; p. 3 Roberto de Gugliemo/Photo Researchers, Inc.; pp. 4-5 © Pat O'Hara/CORBIS; p. 6 Digital Vision; p. 7 (left) Brand X Pictures/Alamy, (right) © Wally Eberhart/Visuals Unlimited; p. 8 (left) © Gerome Wyckoff/Earth Scenes; pp. 8-9 © Jim Sugar/CORBIS; p. 9 (top) Omni Photo Communications Inc./Index Stock Imagery; p. 10 (top) © E. R. Degginger/Earth Scenes, (bottom left, bottom center, bottom right) © Wally Eberhart/Visuals Unlimited; p. 11 Panoramic Images/ Getty Images; p. 12 (left) © Wolfgang Kaehler/CORBIS, (right) Photodisc/Getty Images; p. 13 (top) Fotos and Photos/Index Stock Imagery, (bottom) © Annie Griffiths Belt/CORBIS; p. 14 (top) © Breck Kent/Earth Scenes, (bottom) James Blank/Index Stock Imagery; p. 15 (top left) © E. R. Degginger/Earth Scenes, (top right, center left, center right, bottom left, bottom right) © Breck Kent/Earth Scenes; p. 16 © Peter Johnson/CORBIS; p. 17 (all) © Breck Kent/Earth Scenes; p.18 © Anthony Bannister, Gallo Images/CORBIS; p. 19 Victor Boswell/National Geographic/Getty Images; p. 20 (left) Steve Sant/Alamy, (right) photolibrary.com pty. ltd./Index Stock Imagery; p. 21 (top) © Lester V. Bergman/CORBIS, (bottom) © José Manuel Sanchis Calvete/CORBIS; p. 22 Phil Degginger/Alamy; p. 23 (all) GeoScience Features Picture Library; p. 24 James Lemass/Index Stock Imagery; p. 25 Photodisc/Getty Images; p. 26 (top right) Brand X Pictures, (center left, center right) © Royalty-Free/Corbis, (bottom) Photodisc/Getty Images; pp. 26-27 © Royalty-Free/Corbis; p. 29 Photodisc/Getty Images

ISBN 978-1-4207-0336-8

Printed by Nordica International Ltd.
Manufactured in Guangzhou, China
January, 2010
Nordica Job#: 01-18-10
Sundance/Newbridge PO#: 225780

Cover photo: Quartz crystals found in Brazil

Table of Contents

Good in the Badlands

The landscape looks lonely and bare. Tall mountains with jagged edges rise above steep canyons. Dry and dusty rock stretches as far as the eye can see. In the summer, too little water and too much sun make it a hot, barren place. The Lakota Indians used to call the area *mako sica*, meaning "land bad."

The name still fits today. But Badlands National Park in South Dakota isn't viewed so poorly anymore. The rough and rocky hills are a great source of information for scientists. And they're proof that the rocks on Earth hold amazing stories. The trick is to learn enough about them to unlock their secrets.

CHAPTER 1

All About Rocks

So what, exactly, is a rock? It may seem like a silly question to ask. After all, you've seen thousands of rocks in your lifetime. But even though you've seen them, there still may be a lot you don't know about them. For example, did you know that some rocks are formed from very hot liquid inside of the earth?

What a Rock Is Not

As you've probably noticed, a **rock** isn't alive. That's because it's a solid object that is made up of one or more minerals. What's a **mineral?** A mineral is a piece of matter found in nature that is not, and never was, alive.

Some rocks are made up of one mineral, but most are made up of many minerals that have joined together. Just like toppings on your favorite pizza, some minerals are very easy to see in rock, while others are mixed in so well you can barely tell that they are there.

So why are minerals in a rock so important? By examining the minerals, scientists can figure out what kind of rock it is and even how it was formed.

Minerals in a rock are similar to the toppings on a pizza.

Three Types of Rock

Even though there are billions of rocks in the world, they are grouped into three main types: **igneous, sedimentary,** and **metamorphic.** A rock is classified into one of these types based on how it was formed.

Igneous Rock

The word igneous (IG-nee-uhs) actually means "fire-made." This is a good name for these rocks. Why? Because they are formed when very hot, liquid matter from deep within the earth–called **magma**–cools and hardens. Igneous rock can form above or below the earth's surface.

Diorite

Diorite has time to form large grains because it cools slowly beneath Earth's surface. Obsidian cools above Earth's surface, so its tiny grains make it smooth and glassy.

When igneous rock forms *below* the earth's surface, the magma has time to cool more slowly. This allows the grains, or **crystals,** in the rock to become larger because they have a longer time to form.

Sometimes, however, magma rises quickly to the surface of the earth. When this happens, it pushes the earth's crust up and creates a volcano. When magma erupts, or shoots out of a volcano, it is called **lava.** Lava cools and hardens very quickly, especially if it flows into water. Igneous rocks that form when lava cools quickly tend to have smaller crystals than igneous rocks that cool more slowly underground.

Obsidian

Sedimentary Rock

Unlike igneous rock, sedimentary rock forms more by a settle and squeeze process. Tiny pieces of sand, shells, and other bits of earth, called sediment, constantly settle to the ground or the bottom of lakes, rivers, and oceans. Eventually, layers upon layers of sediment pile on top of each other. The bottom layers of sediment get squeezed together with great weight and pressure. Over a long period of time, they actually cement together to form sedimentary rock. When they remain undisturbed, the bottom layers of sedimentary rock are older than the layers on the top.

There are many different types of sedimentary rock.

You have probably heard of the Grand Canyon. It is made up of sedimentary rock. Once squeezed together, these different layers look like colored lines, or stripes, running across the rock. It's just like when you cut a slice of cake that is made with frosting and fruit; all of the different layers look like stripes.

BLUE PLANET Note

The Grand Canyon is one of the seven natural wonders of the world. Close to 5 million people go to see it every year!

Rare Fossil Finds

Some sedimentary rocks are very special. That's because they contain clues about the history of the earth. These clues are called **fossils.** Fossils are the remains or signs of organisms that lived and died long ago.

So what can fossils show us? Most of the time, fossils include things such as leaves, teeth, bones, eggs, and even just footprints. But in some rare cases, whole animals have been preserved.

Not all dead plants or animals turn into fossils. Most dead organisms decay, are eaten, or are destroyed by weather or other forces. But sometimes an organism, or a piece of one, is covered quickly by sediment. Then it may be preserved for a very long time. This makes the undisturbed layers of sedimentary rock a good place to find fossils.

Fossils like this fern and these trilobites are found in sedimentary rock.

T. rex fossil

BLUE PLANET Note

Scientists who study fossils are called **paleontologists.** But remember, you don't have to be a scientist to find a fossil. Fossils have been found on every continent on Earth, maybe even in your own state!

Remember, fossils are special discoveries, and they are exciting to find because they can help us understand how the earth has changed over time. They can tell us what types of plants and animals have come and gone and help us put together the puzzle of how our Earth has changed.

Metamorphic Rock

Metamorphic means "changed in form," so it would be a good guess to think that a metamorphic rock used to be something else! And that is just the case. Metamorphic rocks form below the surface when extreme heat and pressure change existing rocks into other types of rocks.

How can this happen? The minerals in the existing rocks change when other substances around the rocks are forced by heat or pressure to come together.

Gneiss

Pemaquid Point Lighthouse in Maine sits on layers of the metamorphic rock gneiss.

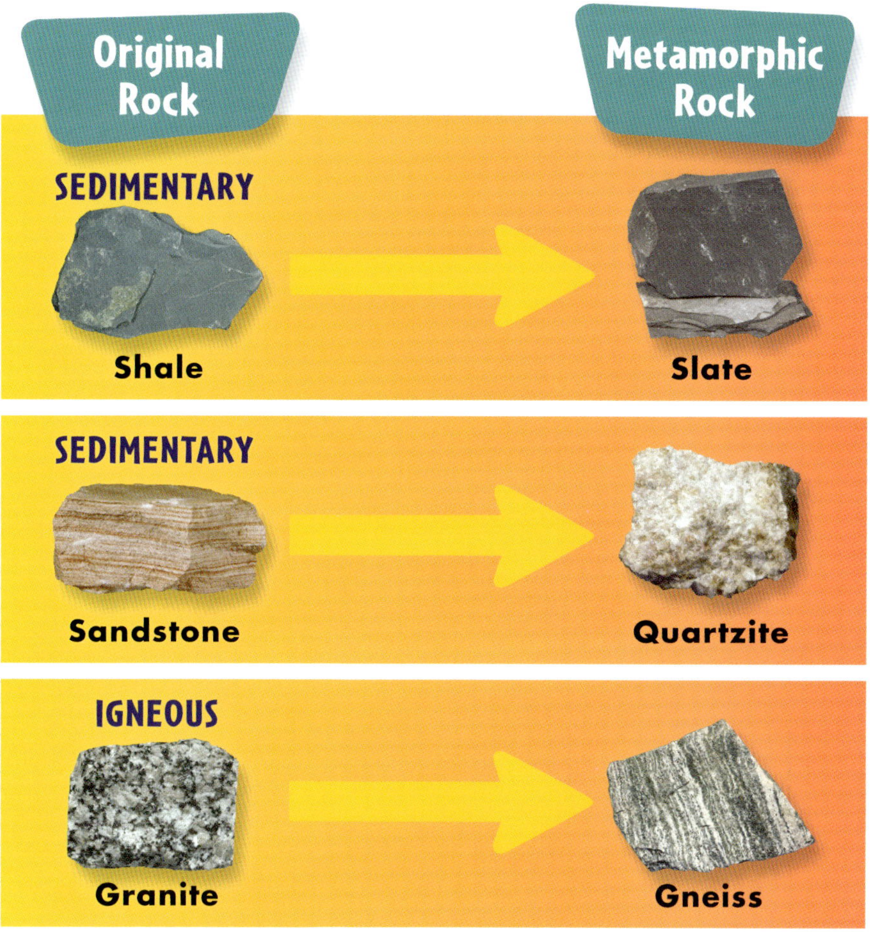

Metamorphic rocks are formed from different types of rocks.

Many metamorphic rocks have a different look and feel than the rocks that formed them. Granite is an igneous rock that usually has big grains because it cools slowly. It also has different minerals such as quartz and mica. However, extreme heat and pressure can turn granite into a metamorphic rock called gneiss (NEYES). Gneiss has some of the same minerals as the granite that formed it. But it looks different. Its minerals are flattened out, so gneiss breaks cleanly along those mineral bands.

The Rock Cycle

Do you ever wonder why we never seem to run out of rocks? It may seem like another silly question, but we never run out of them because of something called the **rock cycle.** What's that? Well, the rock cycle is a slow, never-ending process in which rocks continue to change into other types of rocks.

Here's where it gets a little tricky. Both igneous and sedimentary rock can change through heat and pressure into metamorphic rock. A metamorphic rock can be changed into another metamorphic rock or melted into an igneous rock. Both metamorphic and igneous rock can be broken down into tiny bits of sediment and eventually become sedimentary rock.

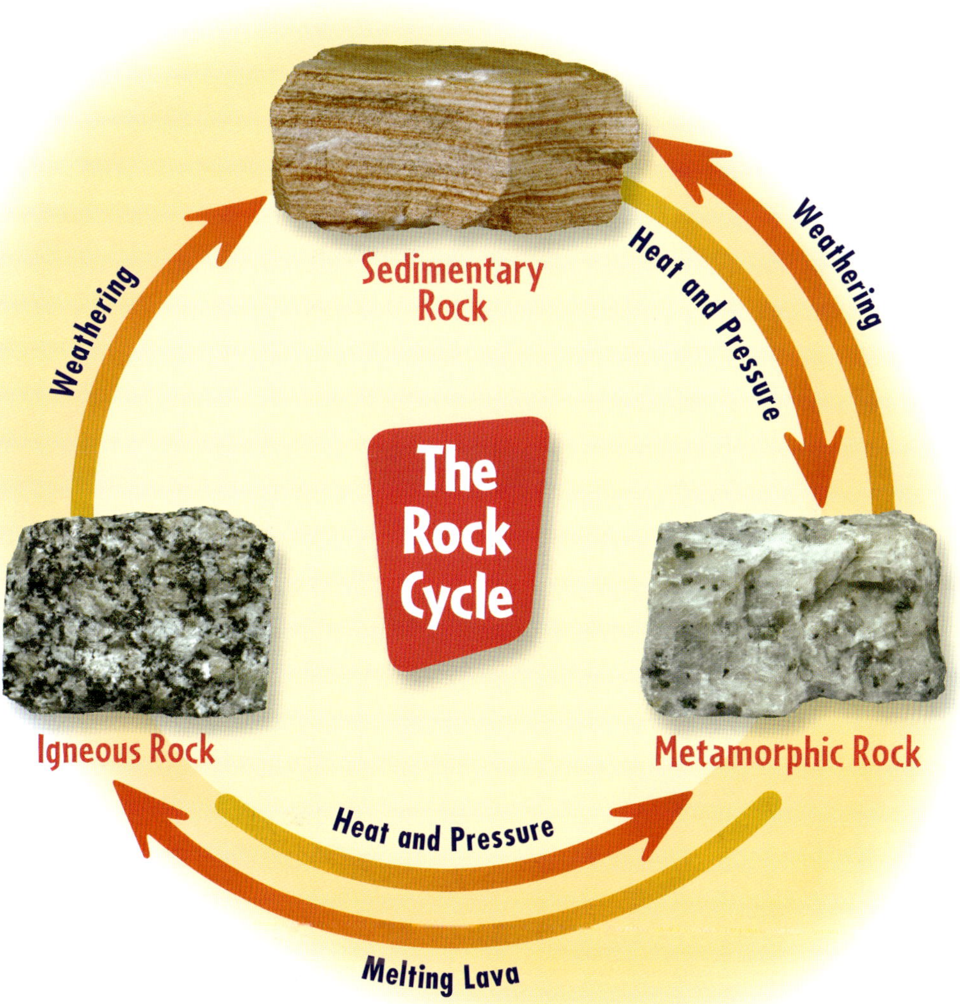

The bottom line is that the rock cycle never stops—it's the earth's version of recycling! Just like when you send a glass bottle to be recycled and it gets changed into another type of glass, the earth takes existing rocks and reuses them to make new rocks. So, a rock you find today probably looked a lot different a long time ago, and it may continue to change over time.

CHAPTER 2

Mountains of Minerals

Geologists, or scientists who study rocks, have identified over 3,000 different minerals! One of the most valuable and the hardest of all of these minerals is the diamond. Because they are so hard, diamonds are sometimes used to cut things.

Identifying Minerals

So how in the world do **geologists** tell all 3,000 minerals apart? Luckily, they can compare the physical properties of minerals to make sense of them all. **Physical properties** of an object can be things such as color and shape. There are dozens of physical properties that are helpful in identifying minerals. So let's take a look at a few.

Color

The first physical property you may notice when you look at a rock is its color. Unfortunately, color is not always a helpful physical property because many minerals you find in rocks have the same color. Sometimes the same mineral can have a few different colors, and some minerals have no color at all!

Quartz comes in different colors. This citrine is a yellowish piece of quartz.

Streak

Since color is not always reliable, another way to identify a mineral involves a **streak** test. A streak is the mark that is left when a mineral is scratched across a light-colored surface. A rock will leave a specific color of streak depending on the minerals it is made of.

BLUE PLANET Note

Don't be fooled! Pyrite is gold in color, but it leaves a black streak, proving it is not the valuable mineral gold. But so many people have mistaken it for real gold that pyrite is now called "fool's gold"!

Luster

Luster is a physical characteristic that describes what the surface of a mineral looks like. Most minerals can be defined as shiny metallics or nonmetallics. Graphite and galena are minerals that have a metallic luster.

Geologists use lots of words to describe a mineral's luster. *Waxy* means the mineral's surface looks like it was made of wax. *Clear* means it looks like glass or crystal.

Hardness

It may sound strange, but not all minerals are "hard as rock"! Some minerals are softer than others, and a scratch test can help tell them apart. If you scratch two minerals together, the harder mineral will leave a mark on the softer one. For example, mica is known to be a very soft mineral, so it is easily scratched.

Another way to test **hardness** is to scratch a mineral with your fingernail, a penny, or a nail. If none of those items scratch the mineral, the mineral is said to be harder than all of those things. Quartz is a hard mineral that will not be scratched by many testers.

Quartz (on left) is a hard mineral that cannot be scratched by the softer mineral pyrite (on right).

Mohs Hardness Scale

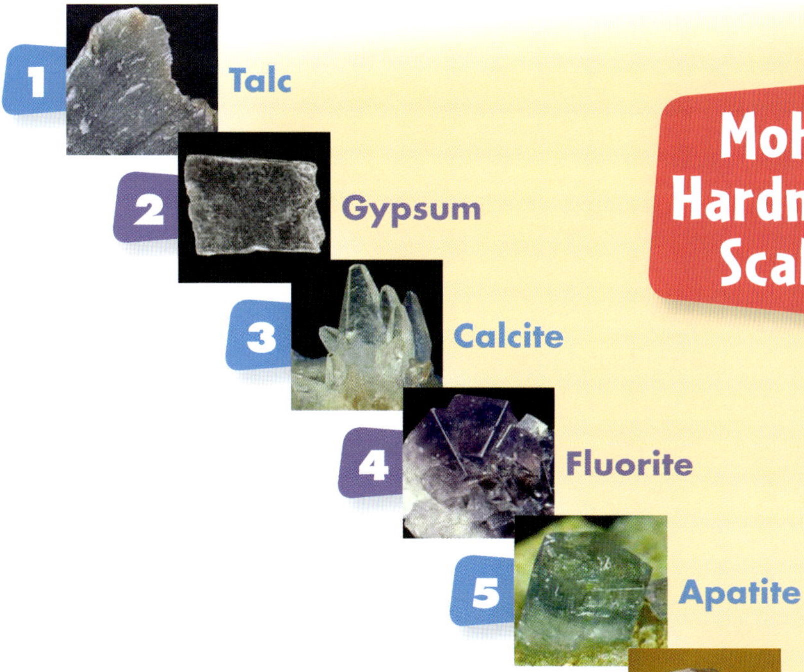

A German scientist by the name of Friedrich Mohs invented a scale to help define the hardness and softness of minerals. On this scale, called **Mohs Hardness Scale,** ten minerals were ranked from softest to hardest and then given a number from one to ten. Number one stands for the softest mineral, talc, and number ten stands for the hardest mineral, diamond. A mineral with a higher number can scratch anything beneath it.

CHAPTER 3

A Million and One Uses

Minerals—you sit on them and wear them. You look at them and eat them. You can even build with them. Just look at the Massachusetts State House in Boston. Its dome was originally coated in copper. Then in 1874, a layer of 23-karat gold was added, giving the State House its unique appearance.

Using Rocks and Minerals

There are so many uses for minerals in our world that it is easy to lose count! In fact, you probably don't even realize how many rocks and minerals you encounter every day.

The most obvious use of rocks and minerals is in the construction of buildings, houses, roads, and sidewalks. For example, rocks such as gravel and limestone, and minerals such as gypsum, are used to make cement and other building materials.

Gems are valuable minerals that have been cut and polished to look their best. Diamonds, rubies, sapphires, and emeralds are the most precious gems. Along with other less valuable gems, they are used to make beautiful jewelry. In fact, gems are usually set within even more minerals, such as silver and gold!

BLUE PLANET Note

The Imperial State Crown, which is part of the Crown Jewel Collection in the United Kingdom, has over 3,000 precious stones in it, including diamonds, sapphires, emeralds, and rubies!

They're Everywhere!

See that pencil on your desk? It contains a mineral called graphite. The chalk up at the blackboard? Calcium carbonate. The silver in an earring, the salt on the table, and the mirror in the bathroom? You guessed it! All minerals! The mineral copper is used in the wire that helps bring electricity to a TV, a computer, and a stereo.

Did you know that minerals also help take care of you? Fluorite makes the fluoride in your toothpaste that helps keep your teeth cavity-free. The lead in an apron protects you when you have an X-ray taken.

Rock Hounds Unite!

A **rock hound** is someone who collects, studies, and identifies all types of rock samples–just for fun! Not sure you're there yet? Think of all you've learned about rocks. You now know what rocks are made of, and you know they are constantly changing. You also know that some rocks are more valuable than others. Some rocks even give clues to past life.

So, the next time you are outside, take a look around. If you find some special rocks, use your new rock hounding skills to investigate them a little further. After all, you never know, a little piece of history may be just a stone's throw away!

Finder File Edit View Go Window Help

Blue Planet E-Diary Blog

BLUE PLANET E-Diary

Tuesday: Writing Assignment

Convince your friends to have a rockin' good time!

Everyone benefits when real scientists take time out from their research to share their knowledge in the classroom.

Imagine that a famous geologist is coming to your school to speak about fossils, rocks, and minerals. How would you convince your friends to stay after school to hear his talk?

Write two paragraphs in support of the event. First, explain why you think it might be important to learn more about the topic. Then try to convince your friends why you think it will be interesting to hear about it from an expert in the field!

posted by BluePlanetXpert / 3:45 PM / Comments 0

Thursday 12:45 PM

Instant Message

Subject:
Rocks are important!

>rockhoundz: Are rocks and minerals really that important?

BluePlanetXpert: Of course! Think of how many ways we use them...from bikes and buildings to coins and cars. Minerals are even in the food you eat!

>rockhoundz: Why are gems so expensive?

BluePlanetXpert: They're the rarest minerals... and when they're cut and polished they can also be the most beautiful!

Blue Planet Chat Room

Subject:
A Rockin' Good Time!

>rockhoundz: Hey . . . I have to convince you guys to come hear the geology speaker. What would you want to ask him about?

trackman2: Fossils!

Beanygirl: How do you get to be a geologist?

Dudestar: Are moon rocks different from the rocks on Earth?

Glossary

crystals minerals with a regular, repeating geometric shape

fossils the remains or signs of past life often found within sedimentary rock

gems minerals that are cut and polished and often used to make jewelry

geologists scientists who study rocks to learn about the earth's history and processes

hardness a physical property of a mineral; a mineral's resistance to being scratched

igneous rock that is formed when hot, liquid matter (lava or magma) cools below or above the surface of the earth

lava hot, liquid magma that breaks to the surface of the earth

luster a physical property of minerals that describes the look of the mineral in light

magma a hot liquid that flows far below the surface of the earth

metamorphic rock formed when extreme heat and pressure change existing rocks into other types of rocks

mineral a naturally occurring solid piece of matter that is not, and was never, alive

Mohs Hardness Scale a scale developed to classify the relative hardness of minerals

paleontologists scientists who study fossils

physical properties characteristics of something that allow for classification

rock a solid piece of matter made up of one or more minerals

rock cycle the process through which one type of rock is changed, over time, into another type of rock

rock hound a person who collects and studies rocks as a hobby

sedimentary rock that forms when bits of sand, clay, and other sediments build up and cement together under intense weight and pressure

streak the colored mark a mineral leaves when scratched across a surface

Index